D0908131

BODY ARTS

THE HISTORY OF TATTOOING AND BODY MODIFICATION™

THE CULTURE OF BODY PIERCING

Don Rauf

Rosen
YA™
New York

Published in 2019 by The Rosen Publishing Group, Inc.
29 East 21st Street, New York, NY 10010

First Edition

Cataloging-in-Publication Data

Names: Rauf, Don.
Title: The culture of body piercing / Don Rauf.
Description: New York : Rosen Publishing, 2019 ¡ Series: Body arts: the history of tattooing and body modification | Includes bibliographical references and index. | Audience: Grades 9–12.
Identifiers: ISBN 9781508180678 (library bound) | ISBN 9781508180685 (pbk.)
Subjects: LCSH: Body piercing—Juvenile literature. | Body marking—Juvenile literature. | Body art—Juvenile literature.
Classification: LCC GN419.25 R38 2019 | DDC 391.6'5—dc23

Manufactured in the United States of America

CONTENTS

INTRODUCTION

et's get right to the point—piercings are more popular than ever. Not only are more people getting them, they're getting them on more places on their bodies than ever before. What was once just a modification for the earlobe has spread to almost every part of the ear, the nose, the lips, the eyebrow, tongue, and belly button. Multiple piercings in the ear have become a hot trend. Celebrities such as Scarlett Johansson know that a "well-curated" ear can really turn heads in the worlds of fashion and entertainment. Piercings are so popular now that the Traditional Tattoo shop in San Luis Obispo, California, says that when it holds a sale, it can do two hundred to three hundred piercings in a single day. In 2016, Racked .com (a site for retail news, fashion happenings, and other information) published a statistic showing that 83 percent of people had pierced ears.

In 2017, the American Academy of Pediatrics recognized that piercings had become so sought after by teenagers that the organization issued its first clinical report on the topic. The report cited a Pew Research Center study finding that an estimated 23 percent of eighteen- to twenty-nine-year-olds had piercings in

Body art, including tattoos and piercings, is more popular than ever. What was once considered a fringe practice has grown into a more acceptable form of self-expression.

locations other than an earlobe. A few generations ago, body piercings for men and women were thought of as customs for delinquents, punks, sailors, and troublemakers. The American Academy of Pediatrics observed, however, that the trend has now gone "mainstream"—although it said it might still be linked to high-risk behavior.

The practice itself is an ancient one, dating as far back as 2000 BCE. Its long history and link to tribal cultures are part of the appeal for some young participants.

Getting a piercing may make them feel part of a tribe, but it is also a way of giving themselves distinct identities.

Because it is a minor surgical procedure, piercing comes with some health risks, and those who pursue it have to take care to make sure the modification is done professionally and with an attention to absolute cleanliness. Equipment that is not properly sterilized can lead to infections and the possible transmission of blood-borne disease.

As more people have gotten body modifications, employers and schools have become more open toward them. Still, some institutions continue to hold a negative view of those who display piercings and tattoos, and that resistance can influence where people work or learn.

Overall, though, the trend is toward greater acceptance, and as we begin the new millennium, the ancient culture of body piercing appears to be poised to continue and gradually change what have been accepted normal societal norms.

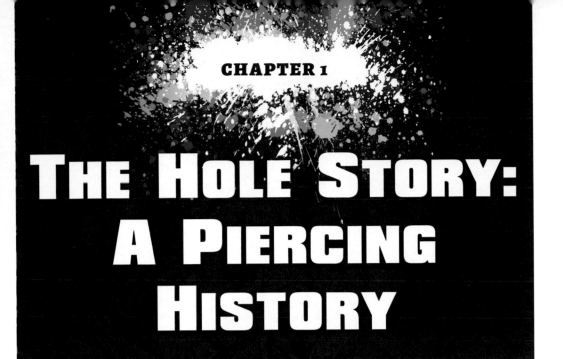

CHAPTER 1

THE HOLE STORY: A PIERCING HISTORY

Body piercing is often thought of as a modern practice. Celebrities such as Christina Aguilera, Britney Spears, Rihanna, Drew Barrymore, Lady Gaga, Kristen Stewart, and Pink all show off their body jewelry. Male celebrities, too, have been jumping on the piercing bandwagon—several have gotten nipple piercings, including basketball star Dennis Rodman, singer Lenny Kravitz, and rock guitarist Dave Navarro. These body modifications are seen as edgy, cool, and current. But poking holes in our bodies to hold jewelry or other adornments is actually an ancient art form.

EARLY MAN AND BODY MODIFICATIONS

Found frozen in the Ötzal Alps along the Italian-Austrian border, Ötzi the Iceman is Europe's oldest-known natural mummy. For one so old, he sported what some consider

The earlobe piercing is common today but the tradition dates back thousands of years. Ötzi, the five thousand year old mummy found frozen in a European glacier, had sizable holes in his lobes suitable for sporting plugs.

a modern look. The five-thousand-year-old traveler had stretched earlobes, with holes measuring about one-third of an inch, indicating that he wore some sort of earring or ear plug.

At the Penn Museum in Philadelphia, a clay head of a four-thousand-year-old female figurine from Iran displays multiple piercings running up the ridge of both ears (almost like Scarlet Johansson today). In the Republic of Cyprus, in the Mediterranean, archaeologists uncovered a pair of gold earrings dating back

HEALTHY PIERCINGS?

Some piercings are believed to be more than just decorative or symbolic. Although the theories have not yet been proven by modern medical science, some believe that certain body modifications can boost health:

Nose rings. In Ayurvedic medicine, a holistic healing system that dates back thousands of years in India, nose rings are said to be able to reduce the pain that women experience during menstruation. That is why Indian women are often wearing nose rings. Some uphold that a pierced nose with a gold ring will constantly stimulate the stomach, drawing in energy toward digestion, immunity, and the reproductive organs.

Earrings. Acupuncture is the practice of inserting thin needles into the body at specific points to relieve pain, treat a disease, or anesthetize a body part during surgery. Some acupuncturists say that there are more than two hundred acupuncture points in the ear and that certain earrings may relieve migraines and allergy symptoms. Some specifically seek out piercing part of the ear called the daith (the ear's most inner cartilage fold) for migraine relief.

Navel rings. If a woman is trying to get pregnant, some acupuncturists recommend not having a navel piercing because it interrupts a flow of energy that helps with fertility.

more than two thousand years. All these artifacts demonstrate how early humans sought to enhance their bodies through piercing.

While the Bible makes reference to this body modification, it also condemns it. In the Book of Genesis, Abraham's servant gave Rebekah a nose ring called a *shanf*. Scientists have uncovered Hebrew body jewelry (used for piercings) in archaeological digs across modern-day Israel.

Yet some Christians and Jews hold that the practice goes against God's will—it is wrong to desecrate or mutilate the body. In the Bible, the passage Leviticus 19:28 reads: "You shall not make any cuttings in your flesh for the dead, nor tattoo any marks on you: I am the Lord."

Other religions hold similar beliefs and view piercings as ungodly and vulgar. Some, however, such as the Hindu faith, perceive piercing as a way to express spirituality. Many spiritual individuals defend the art as a form of self-expression that is part of the human experience.

A TRIBAL TRADITION

Throughout history, ethnic groups have attached different meanings to bodily punctures. Many of these traditions have been practiced for thousands of years. In Southeast Alaska, a native tribe called the Tlingit people have used ear piercing as a way to denote a person's standing in society. The tribe's women would hang ornaments of shell, stone, and teeth from their ears. Tlingit females also wear nose rings as symbols of prestige. Both males and females pierce the septum (the partition that separates the nostrils) as well.

Today, young people have taken to septum piercing, but it has been a long-standing ritual among many tribes across the globe. Often, warriors plug their septum openings with bone or other material to intimidate enemies. The tribesmen of Papua (western New Guinea) in Indonesia and the nearby Solomon Islands look especially fierce with huge, sharp boar tusks jutting out from their nostrils. The bigger the adornments, the greater the status. Asmat

Tribes have practiced body modification for tens of thousands of years. To look more fierce, a Tlingit warrior of the Northwest might wear a bone ring through the septum.

tribe members in Papua craft enormous bone plugs from pig legs that measure as much as one inch (2.5 centimeters) in diameter. Somehow, they fit the large bones through their septa. In the Pacific Northwest, the Shawnees and many other American tribes have engaged in septum piercing. The Nez Percé tribe derived its name from the French for "pierced nose."

Nostril piercing can be found in the cultures of ancient Mexico and India as well. Among certain people of India, wearing a nose ring continues to be a way to pay homage to Parvati, a Hindu goddess who represents marriage.

LIP SERVICE

Oral piercings are common among many African tribes. For the Dogon people of Africa, lip rings connect to their mythology and represent the creation of speech. In the Makololo tribe, originally from South Africa, women wear plates in their upper lips to enhance their beauty. Typically, a fiancé inserts the plate six months before her marriage. The size of the plate corresponds to the size of the dowry.

The people of the Mayan and Aztec tribes of Mexico and Central America boasted lip piercings adorned with gold or jade and carved with characters from their religion. They also practiced tongue piercing as a way to make a closer connection with their gods.

Until the late 1800s, some native Alaskan men pierced their lips with one plug in the middle or two on either side of the lip.

EAR ENHANCEMENT

In recent years, ear gauging has grown in popularity. For gauging, the earlobes are stretched and large gauges, spools, or plugs are inserted. Again, what might seem new has its roots in ancient cultures. For centuries, the Mayan people have worn ear plugs and spools carved from obsidian (naturally occurring volcanic glass). They varied in size from about a half inch (1.3 cm) to an inch (2.5 cm) in diameter.

Guatama Buddha (depicted here) started the fourth-largest religion in the world in the sixth century BCE. He was known to have very long earlobes with large holes.

Gautama Buddha, the founder of Buddhism, thought to have lived in India from 563 BCE to 483 BCE, was famous for his dramatic earlobes, which dangled to great lengths. He stretched them using heavy gold or other precious stones. Later, when Buddha renounced worldly wealth, he discarded all jewelry and was left with his famous ultra-long lobes. King Tut's mummy revealed that he not only had ear piercings but he also was a member of the stretched lobe club.

The Rapa Nui natives of Easter Island, famed for its mysterious stone sculptures, were known for their far-reaching lobes. In the 1700s, Captain Cook wrote that the islanders' ears were "pierced with large holes,

Women of the nomadic Wodaabe tribe, a subgroup of the Fulani in Africa, may wear several large hoop earrings as part of their courtship rituals.

through which four or five fingers might be thrust with ease." When Christianity spread among the people, the practice quickly died out, however.

For centuries, the Maasai tribes of Kenya have lengthened their earlobes using weights. They widened the holes over time with increasingly larger stones, bundles of twigs, bits of tusk, or until recently, film canisters. The Maasai are known for creating colorful, intricate beadwork that they often loop through their ear holes. Many young Maasai people today now avoid the traditional piercings and choose to live a "modern" life.

In the Fulani tribe in Nigeria and Central Africa, girls receive holes in their ears at age three. As they grow older, many hang elaborate gold hoops from their piercings. In Ethiopia, the women of the Mursi tribe stretch their lobes to fit large wooden "plates." To show they've reached childbearing age, young Mursi females insert a wooden peg through their ears. The people of the Dayak tribe of Borneo attach brass weights to extend their ears—the longer the lobe, the more respected the tribe member. Although it is a dying art, a few modern-day Dayak people have lobes that reach all the way to their shoulders.

Piercing is not just for girls. For the people of the Naga tribes in the northeastern part of India, the ear ceremony is an important rite for young boys about to enter manhood.

A MARK OF MANLINESS?

Roman warriors, including Julius Caesar, are said to have pierced their nipples as a sign of virility and strength. The body modification, shared by the soldiers and their leader, bound the men together.

Legend has it that Egyptian pharaohs may have adorned themselves with navel rings as a sign of masculine courage and power. Any other Egyptian male who dared to decorate the belly button would be put to death. Although historical evidence to support this is scarce, some scholars add that a pierced navel may have been a symbol of one's transition from the life on Earth to the life of eternity.

Do today's male celebrities who get nipple piercings also do it as a measure of manliness? Maybe not, but it certainly gets them attention.

SPREADING TO THE WESTERN WORLD

For centuries in Europe, piercings were not common. In the late fourteenth century, however, Isabella of Bavaria promoted a fashion of necklines that plunged so outrageously low that they exposed the breasts. Many wealthy women of the era then pierced their exposed nipples and decorated them with jewels and linked them with strands of pearls or gold chains. In the 1890s, the "bosom ring" echoed the era of Isabella and came back briefly as a fad in London and Paris.

As the cultural and artistic Renaissance gained steam in England in the late fifteenth century, gentlemen began brandishing earrings. Shakespeare, Sir Walter Raleigh, and Francis Drake all wore golden ear jewelry. Of course, pirates and sailors often flaunted earrings as well. As with men who sport them today, the jewelry gave a swashbuckling image and a sense of danger.

Some seamen may have commemorated their first voyage across the equator by getting an earring. Many sailors held the misconception that the ear decoration could cure bad eyesight or protect them from diseases or even drowning. If they did die, a piece of ear jewelry had a practical purpose—it could be sold for enough money to provide a decent burial. Some found another good use for the rings—by attaching a piece of wax to them, the wearer could easily plug his ears to muffle the deafening blast of cannon fire.

A COMEBACK

By the first half of the twentieth century, piercings and tattoos were out of vogue. Overall, they were viewed as body modifications that only criminals or deviants—like gang members, particularly those in biker gangs—might get. Clip-on earrings grew in popularity through the 1930s and 1940s. Still, some viewed women who got their ears pierced as not respectable.

In the latter half of the twentieth century, some young people began to embrace various forms of body modification as an expression of individualism and rebellion.

In the early 1950s, however, the trend slowly gained momentum as young adult females began piercing their ears on their own. Queen Elizabeth II helped pave the way when she got her ears pierced after receiving a pair of diamond earrings as a wedding present. Because no shops existed at the time to do the job, girls would often gather together and take a DIY (do-it-yourself) approach. Using a sewing needle and a cube of ice behind the lobe, they'd perform the task themselves. Gradually, as infections and slip-ups became more common, parents sought out family doctors to do the job, and the number of professional piercers slowly rose.

As often happens in popular culture, what was once considered a subculture grew to become the norm. In the 1960s, many young people were embracing the hippie movement. Young people started this counterculture movement as a call for peace in reaction to the Vietnam War and out of disillusionment with an increasingly materialistic society following World War II. They were rebelling with rock music, long hair, drug use, and protests. Along with tattoos of peace signs, religious symbols, and other designs, hippies embraced piercings. Most notably, hippies brought nose piercings to the Western world. As they sought enlightenment in Indian culture and traditions, they embraced this body modification.

In the 1970s and '80s, the punk rock movement adapted piercing as a means of rebellion. Like hippies, punks were antiestablishment, but they believed In a more aggressive approach to change. Whereas hippies were all about peace, love, and mellowness, punks were about anarchy and disruption. They styled their hair into Mohawks or shaved their heads. They wore torn clothing and listened to loud music. Not only did they get nose and ear piercings, but they also got tongue, cheek, eyebrow, and many other kinds of piercings. They helped to push piercing to a new level, and in many ways they helped pave the way to make piercing the more mainstream type of body modification it is today.

CHAPTER 2

MODERN MODIFICATIONS: WHY PEOPLE GET PIERCED

In many cultures, piercings have been a part of their heritage and tradition. Throughout history, people have pierced themselves for aesthetic reasons, to decorate their bodies with jewelry, and to make themselves more beautiful. To a large degree, that's why people get pierced today.

Glittering jewels are fashion accessories that can be worn in the ears to make a person stand out. In some cases, jewelry such as diamonds and rare stones indicate a level of class and may convey an image of wealth. The variety of items that people hang from their ears is almost endless, including beads, tassels, hoops, charms, and light stones.

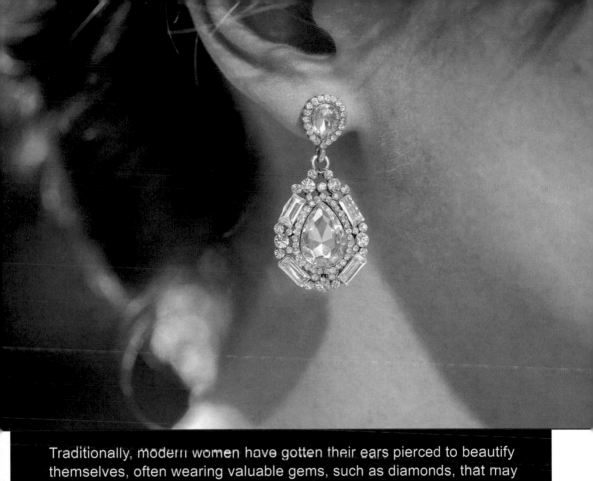

Traditionally, modern women have gotten their ears pierced to beautify themselves, often wearing valuable gems, such as diamonds, that may convey wealth.

Fashion and beauty experts understand how certain styles can also complement one's features. Long vertical earrings, for instance, can provide a narrowing effect for someone with a round face. Some will adorn a bodily feature to call attention to its beauty. Belly button piercings are one of the most popular piercings among women today. Some fashion experts say that the trend began when the actress Alicia Silverstone rocked a pierced navel in the 1993 music video for the Aerosmith song "Cryin'." That year, the model Christy Turlington walked the runway at a London fashion show, flaunting her adorned belly button before the crowds.

FOLLOWING THE TRENDS

Often, a beauty trend will be established once celebrities embrace it. Among both men and women, the ancient art of nipple piercing has been on the rise. Mic.com, a website that touts a readership of tens of millions of young people, called nipple piercing 2016's biggest trend. Kendall and Kylie Jenner, Bella Hadid, and Rihanna have them, as do Dennis Rodman and Mötley Crüe's Tommy Lee. Depending on the wearer, these piercings can accentuate femininity or masculinity. In an interview with Mic.com, professional piercer Cassie Lopez said that while nipple piercings were more popular than ever, they're also easy to hide when one doesn't want the world to know they're there.

Another trend reported on by *Bustle* magazine is constellation piercings—a small cluster of earrings, like stars that dot the lobe or upper ear. Ear suspenders have become another fad—they are little decorative bars that hook into the top of the earlobe. Other styles are earring jackets that cover the bottom of the ear, ear cuffs that clip on to the top of the ear, and cartilage piercings—a popular choice is a bar running through two openings in the upper ear.

Bustle also reported that certain piercing trends that were popular in the 1990s, including navel piercing, are making a comeback. These include septum piercing, hanging a ring from the divider that separates the nostrils. In 2016, the *New York Times* called a septum piercing the newest "it" accessory for young adults seeking to make a fashion statement. Musicians Rihanna, Kat Graham, and Ellie Goulding all have been showing off these adornments. The *Times* pointed out that it appeared to be a generational thing that could distinguish the younger

Piercings today have gone beyond the ear and nose—eyebrows, lips, belly buttons, and tongues are all popular sites on the body for self-adornment.

generation. They want to claim it as their own. It's about the freedom to do as one wishes and be different.

One twenty-year-old man with a septum piercing said,

I got my piercing for almost entirely aesthetic reasons. I chose the septum in particular because of how it looks. I think it ornaments my face in a symmetrical and flattering way. The practice of facial piercing is also extremely old, and much like tattooing, I think it's a cool way of decorating your body that countless people and cultures have participated in for centuries.

Eyebrow and tongue piercings, which were also popular in the 1990s, have been resurging.

MODERN PRIMITIVISM

Some have labeled this current interest in body modification modern primitivism (or urban primitivism). A book published in 1989 titled *Modern Primitives* spurred interest in the movement; it said people were pursuing body modifications in response to primal urges and paying homage to primitive cultures. Piercings, tattoos, and other body modifications were rituals that could mark personal growth, rites of passage, or spiritual beliefs and provide a connection with the world and others that modern society was lacking. Some piercers light sage, burn candles, and dim the lights to make the whole process more of a ritual and allow clients to focus on the moment.

When individuals get piercings, they may feel as if they are joining an unofficial club of sorts and can feel a sense of belonging with others who also have piercings. It can be a way to feel like one belongs to something greater.

FATHER OF THE MODERN PRIMITIVES

Ronald Loomis, who changed his name to Fakir Musafar, was born on an Indian reservation in South Dakota. He grew up in the 1930s in an area populated by Native American tribes. The elders in these tribes introduced him to the spiritual practice of putting hooks in the skin and body suspension.

A 2012 article in *The Atlantic* traced the practice of body suspension as far back as five thousand years. The earliest form is thought to have originated in India as a type of religious penance. Although for many years Musafar held executive positions in San Francisco advertising agencies and operated his own ad agency in Silicon Valley, he has dedicated his life to the spiritual side of body mutilation and the ritualistic aspects of suspension.

After decades of pursuing piercing, scarification, tattooing, and hook suspension, he became known as the "father of the modern primitives." Now in his late eighties, Musafar has seen more young people participating in suspension for the experience and self-discovery. He is committed to teaching the history of the ritual and sharing the experience as a means to reach a higher spiritual plane.

A few in the modern primitive movement have followed the custom of the Makololo people of South Africa and adopted the practice of stretching their lips with plates. Just as some African tribes would stretch their earlobes and create extra large holes to accommodate large round items, certain body modifiers follow the same practice, wearing large gauges or plugs, often to show respect for this tribal tradition. Flesh tunnels, or large spools that allow for a large hole in the lobe, have caught on in popularity as well.

FOR MAKING A STATEMENT OR MARKING A MILESTONE

Along with wanting to make themselves more attractive, people often get a piercing as a sign of individuality. They want to stand out in a crowd and make a statement that says, "Look at me. I am unique."

There is a sense of edginess and daring still associated with piercings—after all, a piercing was for a long time the domain of pirates and punk rockers. It can be perceived as cool and make a rebellious statement.

For many young women, ear piercing was a rite of passage as they grew up. While it often marked the milestone of leaving girlhood behind and becoming a young woman, girls have been getting pierced ears at younger ages. While it has been common for girls to get their ears pierced in Western culture, boys have increasingly joined. They also often get one as a statement: "I'm an adult now; this is who I am." Some young people may get a piercing when they are just entering adulthood or in their young teens. Some commemorate graduating high school or college.

A fourteen-year-old from Phoenicia, New York, got her nose pierced recently because she said she thought it would help give her confidence. She said that a lot of kids do it because it makes them look older.

For many young women, getting their ears pierced is a rite of passage as they get older. A piercing gun is one method, but customers must always be careful about cleanliness.

A DECISION TO SLEEP ON

The urge to get a piercing can be spontaneous and not always very well thought out. Perhaps a friend got one or you had a sudden urge. Although jumping in and getting a piercing without much thought might

WORKPLACE WORRIES AND SCHOOL RULES

One consideration that anyone thinking of getting a piercing needs to make is how it may affect his or her ability to get and keep a job. A 2017 article in *USA Today* said that a survey of nearly 2,700 people found that three-quarters felt that noticing tattoos and piercings hurt an applicant's chances of being hired during a job interview. More than half said they thought visible body piercings were always inappropriate at work.

Over the years, Starbucks has loosened up its rules and now allows small ear gauges or small nose studs but no septum piercings or tongue studs. Other than traditional ear piercing for females, Disney has set guidelines forbidding all other piercings. Some companies are more accepting. In a 2017 interview on Business.com, Jim Whitehurst, CEO of Redhat, said that his firm wanted people to feel comfortable and free to be who they were, so tattoos and piercings were welcome.

Schools may also have regulations regarding visible body modifications. With piercings, many studs and rings can be removed if working or learning in an environment that upholds strict appearance codes.

be exciting, one can live to regret it later. Religious individuals may realize that it goes against their religion. It's always wise to take some time and consider the pros and cons and seriously ask yourself why you want a piercing.

RECLAIMING ONE'S BODY

A study titled "Modifying the Body: Motivations for Getting Tattooed and Pierced" observed that some women who had suffered abuse used body piercings as a way to reclaim their bodies. Your body is something that is yours and no one else can own it. The research stated that the piercing could "create a new understanding of the injured part of the body and reclaim possession through the deliberate, painful procedure of body modification." For some, a piercing is a path toward healing wounds. Some believe the act of intentionally causing physical harm to oneself can ease internal pain.

The body also releases endorphins in response to pain. Endorphins are morphinelike "feel-good" chemicals in the brain that bring on feelings of pleasure or euphoria when the body is experiencing pain, emotional stress, or strenuous exercise. Endorphins explain what causes the "runner's high," the good feeling that some people get while running. Pierc-

For some, the pain from piercing releases endorphins, chemicals in the body that cause pleasure. They seek out the procedure to experience this euphoria.

ings can induce this feeling as well, and some people return for more and more body modifications just so they can experience this feeling.

An individual may experience an adrenaline rush as well when getting a piercing. Adrenaline is a hormone secreted through the adrenal glands when something threatening or exciting is happening. A surge of adrenaline can make a person feel alive and happy.

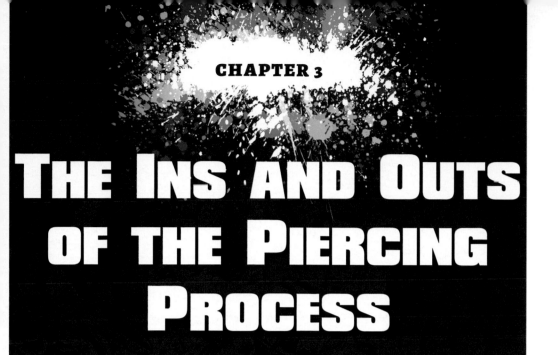

CHAPTER 3

THE INS AND OUTS OF THE PIERCING PROCESS

For those considering piercing their bodies, there are certain factors to consider in the decision-making process. The first one may be age.

While anyone over eighteen is legally considered an adult and can make his or her own decisions, those under eighteen years of age are minors and laws vary from state to state. The National Conference of State Legislators reports that thirty-eight states prohibit body piercing and tattooing minors without parental permission. So for a minor, the choice of getting any body modification involves a serious talk with a parent or guardian. Usually, a minor needs written consent. Many states allow earlobe piercing with parental consent starting at age five. Some state rules require a parent to be in attendance during the procedure.

If a person is of adult age, he or she may have to present a birth certificate or another official form showing proof of age. Some states, such as Idaho, restrict piercing for anyone under the age of fourteen. Mississippi forbids any piercing for minors. Nevada, on the other hand, has no laws about body art. Minnesota specifically prohibits genital or nipple piercings, branding, scarification, suspension, subdermal implantation, micro-dermal implants, or tongue bifurcation on minors.

A WORLD OF CHOICES

When it comes to first steps, the process begins with shopping around. Individuals have to consider the jewelry styles that suit them best. Should the adornment be small and humble or big and flashy? The internet presents thousands of options to explore. In-person visits to jewelry shops, piercing studios, and even large retail stores let potential customers see for themselves what jewelry choices look like on their body. Checking out potential picks up close in a mirror can help clinch a decision. Today, body piercing has gone so mainstream that even Walmart sells nose rings and lip labrets. Walmart offers piercing services, too, but the chain does only ears.

Materials are varied. Choices include surgical steel, titanium, fourteen-karat gold, acrylic, glass, natural stone, and wood. Allergies may factor in to the

The path to a personal piercing begins with shopping around. Seeing how jewelry looks in person—and getting advice from a trusted friend—is a great way to decide.

decision-making process. With a new piercing that isn't quite healed, tissue can have a negative reaction. Nickel is a common culprit when it comes to irritation and can turn the skin green or black. It is estimated that up to 17 percent of women and 3 percent of men are allergic to nickel, and metal hypersensitivity may continue after the piercing has healed. Gold, bone, and wood can also cause trouble in an early piercing. Watch for itching, redness, rash, dry patches, and swelling of the skin.

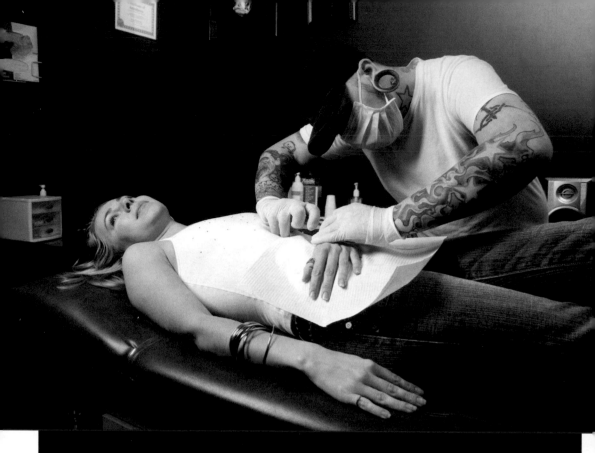

Piercings can involve some pain, which often depends on the body location. Some describe the belly button procedure as feeling like a small pinch.

MAKE TIME FOR THE PAIN

For a person new to the whole process, it's a good idea to ask someone you know and trust who already has a piercing what it's like. One of the top questions is "Does it hurt?" With any piercing, there's the initial sharp pain of the prick followed by longer, duller pain that follows the procedure. Some practitioners will take anesthetic measures to numb the skin beforehand, using ice, rubbing alcohol, numbing sprays or creams, or Tylenol, for example. A new piercing can create mild pain and soreness, redness, and swelling for twenty-four to forty-eight hours. Complete healing can take even longer. Most earlobe piercings heal fully in four to six weeks. A nipple can take up to six months and a navel can take up to a year.

On the pain scale, an earlobe piercing is relatively quick and might be the least severe (although there will still be some pain.) The piercing shop Blue Banana polled its customers to gauge which piercings hurt most and least and found that the earlobe gave the lowest level of grief. Many compared it to a bee sting lasting a few seconds. Nostrils, lips, and ear cartilage are considered to be a bit more unpleasant but not too bad. One of the more distressing piercings is the nipple because it's a very sensitive area.

Sophie Dodd wrote of her experience getting a nose piercing on HerCampus.com: "I'm not going to lie: it hurts. I have four piercings on my earlobes and four on my cartilage, and those were nothing compared to a nose piercing: I would give it a 3.5 or 4 out of 5 on a piercing pain scale."

SHOPPING FOR A SHOP

A person you trust with a piercing may not only give advice on the process, he or she may also be able to recommend a reputable piercing establishment (or warn you about any place where he or she had a bad experi-

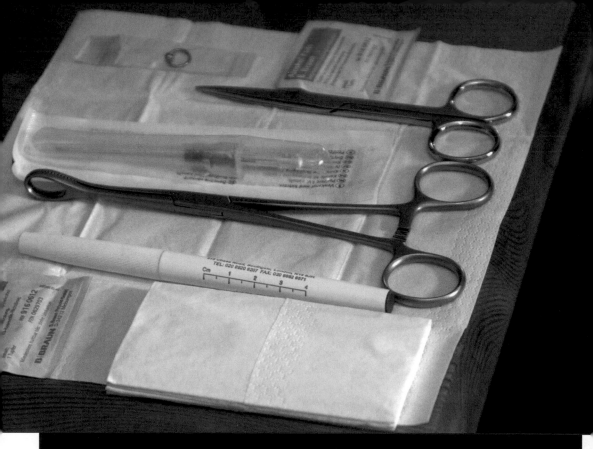

Cleanliness is extremely important when it comes to body modification. Piercers must carefully sterilize their tools to prevent infections in customers.

ence). Some doctors perform ear piercings, but it's not a common choice. At the top of your checklist, make sure the piercer maintains high standards of cleanliness. Typically, piercers sterilize their equipment in an autoclave, a container similar to a pressure cooker that uses high temperatures and pressure to kill bacteria and germs. Check that the staff washes hands, wears gloves, and keeps all equipment totally clean.

Many states require piercers to be licensed, which indicates that they have met certain quality standards.

A professional piercer may hold certification with the Association of Professional Piercers (APP), which demonstrates that the piercer has completed at least a year-long apprenticeship.

In general, more experience means better results. Oregon, for example, requires practitioners to have hundreds of hours of training and pass written exams before being licensed for specific types of body art. According to a 2017 report from the Pew Charitable Trusts, Maryland does not license body artists, though it requires them to use sterile instruments, wash their hands, wear disposable gloves during procedures, and cleanse customers' skin. These operations must also keep three years of customer records and make them available to health officers if requested. Check with your state government to get any available information about licenses for piercing shops and their status.

After pinpointing a potential service, pay a visit to see how the operation works. Ask questions about how they maintain proper hygiene and sterilize their equipment.

Cost can be a deciding factor as well. Make sure you know all the charges up-front. A standard ear perforation costs from twenty to fifty-five dollars, according to the consumer website CostHelper Health. The price of nostril piercing ranges from thirty to sixty-five dollars. A studio may tack on the cost of some standard piece of jewelry and an aftercare service charge. A gratuity for the piercer of 5 to 15 percent is common practice.

NEEDLE VERSUS GUN

Customers may get their earlobes pierced with a needle, but nowadays a piercing gun is frequently the tool of choice, especially at the mall. Usually just used for the lobe, this device resembles a glue gun or staple gun. Using a spring action, the gun "shoots" a piercing stud into the lobe as it snaps a backing in

Mall jewelry shops frequently use piercing guns for speed and efficiency, but they are not always sanitized in an appropriate way and can transmit blood-borne pathogens.

place. The gun is reusable because no part of the machine comes in contact with the ear. The earlobe touches a disposable cartridge containing the starter earring and backing. Older models did not come with a disposable cartridge and were difficult to clean.

Although stores will disinfect their guns, piercing guns can never be completely sterilized because they are made of plastic. The APP does not support the use of piercing guns because they can't be sterilized using APP-approved equipment, such as an autoclave. Since the guns are usually made of plastic, they would melt in an autoclave.

A 2015 article in *Good Housekeeping* and other sources recommend the needle over the gun. Not only is the gun more prone to spreading disease, it can be more painful and damaging to the tissue as it forcefully punches a post through the lobe. The hollow needle easily pushes through the tissue with much less trauma.

Needles are single use and disposable to assure cleanliness. They should be taken out of the disposable packaging.

WHAT GETTING A PIERCING IS LIKE

When a person settles on a piercing shop and is ready to move ahead with the body modification, the first step is filling out paperwork. In most cases, a customer signs verification that he or she understands the possible risks

GAUGING THE RISKS

Why can gauging, or gradually increasing the size of a piercing hole to fit larger jewelry, be a bigger decision than getting a piercing? Because gauging holes are bigger and require a lot more than a hole being made. It's not an overnight process. Weeks or years may be necessary to reach the desired size to accommodate a plug. The process requires making a hole (typically in an earlobe) larger and larger to fit a big plug. Some wait eight to ten weeks or longer between stretches to make sure the tissue recovers. Going too fast can tear tissue, cause scarring, and make it more difficult to ever shrink back up, if that is desired.

There is no guarantee that earlobes will return to their normal size on their own once gauged—so potential permanence should be figured into the decision-making process. A visit to a plastic surgeon might be the only solution. A common stretching technique uses a taper, which is thin on one end and fat on the other, and usually made of acrylic or stainless steel. After putting a lubricant (such as vitamin E oil) on the tip, an individual slowly rotates the taper into an initial size and then inserts a plug. Over time, the gauge size on the jewelry can increase. As with all body modifications, a professional can help make sure nothing drastic happens.

involved in the procedure and indicates any health issues or medications being taken. By signing a form giving consent to the piercing procedure, customers acknowledge that they understand what they are getting into and they "hold harmless" the piercer from any legal action. Typically, a piercer will copy any identification papers and have a parent complete any required paperwork as well.

The customer either has to bring jewelry for the piercing or pick out a piece. The shop professional may advise a starter piece of jewelry just to get the piercing going—like a placeholder until the preferred adornment can go in. The piercer will put starter jewelry and any tools he or she may need to use (like ring opening and closing pliers) in the autoclave. Instead of an autoclave, some shops may disinfect with a dry heat sterilizer or chemical bath.

For many procedures, the client sits in a reclining chair (similar to a dentist seat), which helps the customer relax and makes it easier for the professionals to do their job.

The piercer will disinfect the skin where the piercing will be and mark the exact spot with a surgical marker, verifying with the customer that the location is correct. As with any procedure, communication between client and practitioner is key. Asking questions and talking things through can help calm any nervousness.

Often, the piercer slides the jewelry into place as he or she is doing the piercing. A little blood may have

Fans of piercings have to endure a certain amount of pain in the pursuit of beauty. Piercings today are considered very fashionable among models and actresses.

to be cleaned up around the new hole, and the area may become red and tender. The client might feel a little woozy.

When the procedure is completed, the piercer will discuss proper hygiene and aftercare to make sure the customer stays healthy and avoids any problems.

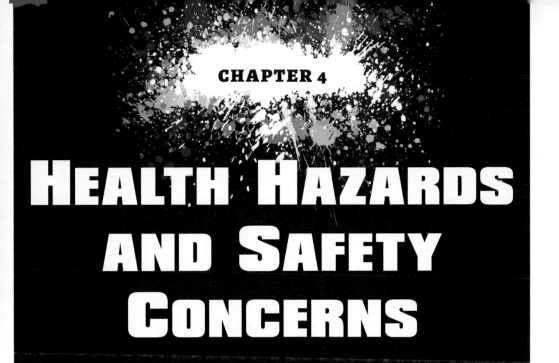

CHAPTER 4

HEALTH HAZARDS AND SAFETY CONCERNS

While most who get piercings do not suffer major health troubles, puncturing holes through the flesh comes with certain health risks. An opening in the skin provides a doorway for germs, bacteria, fungi, and viruses to enter the body.

The biggest way to keep health problems away is through cleanliness. If conditions are not sanitary, a customer runs a risk of getting an infection. Some infections can be easily cured, while others are potentially deadly. Some can start as relatively harmless but then turn lethal if not treated right away. In rare cases, infections lead to blood poisoning or toxic shock syndrome, most commonly caused by staph bacteria but sometimes by strep bacteria.

The healing process may produce some white secretion around a new opening. While that is a natural reaction, the presence of green or yellow pus may signal an infection. If a large enough abscess (collection of pus) builds up, it may have to be surgically drained and can potentially leave a scar.

Professional piercers maintain high levels of hygienic standards to prevent health issues. The APP advises against a do-it-yourself approach—home piercers are unlikely to achieve the same levels of cleanliness as pros, and the odds for a slip-up or accident are much higher for the inexperienced. Using an experienced piercer lowers the chances for disfigurement, scarring, and the formation of cysts under the skin.

AFTERCARE IS KEY

Piercers take time to explain postprocedure treatment because problems can pop up if a new piercing is not kept clean. Customers should follow all postcare instructions carefully. New openings should be gently washed with warm water and a facial cleanser, mild soap, or a saline solution, such as H2Ocean or Recovery Piercing Aftercare Spray. To ensure against infection, a first aid liquid or spray may help, although alcohol and hydrogen peroxide are to be avoided as they can further irritate the skin. Sweat can aggravate the skin as well, so washing after exercise is a must.

The smallest granule of dirt can provoke a reaction if it gets into a still-healing opening. The cleaning ritual may continue for weeks as the healing continues.

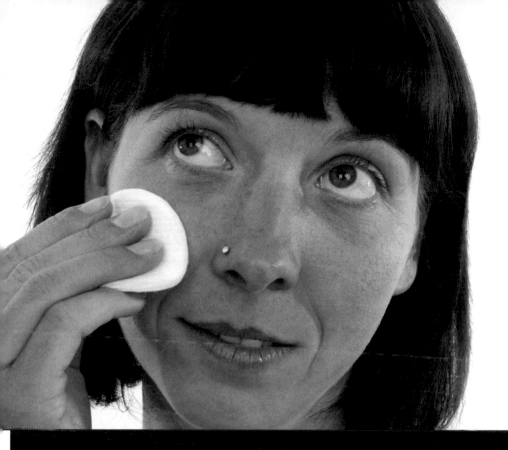

To avoid infections, individuals must keep the skin around their piercing clean. A gentle wash with a mild soap can often do the job.

Touching or rubbing a fresh perforation can spread bacteria and lead to further irritation. It's safest to keep items away from the piercing as well, such as phones, ear buds, glasses, hats, and bike helmets. Those who wear makeup are advised to be careful when using a foundation, concealer, and hairspray as it may disrupt the healing process. Other warnings include: do not get into a hot tub or swim in a pool or lake; stay out of direct sunlight and avoid sunburns; and avoid smoking, drugs, and alcohol.

WHEN THINGS GET SERIOUS

There is no need to freak out over a little redness and tenderness. A bacterial infection may produce a small eruption, but if it is minor, it may be treated at home by continued gentle cleaning and taking ibuprofen or Tylenol to reduce inflammation. Removing the piercing, however, may worsen the condition.

If the pain is ongoing and the opening is producing a yellow or green pus, then an infection may have developed, and a doctor's attention may be needed. A

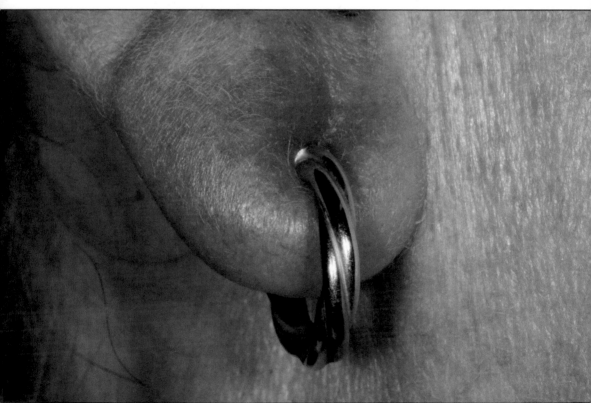

Some redness after a procedure is to be expected, but when the area becomes too inflamed it can be a sign of a bacterial infection, and proper medical attention is required.

fever or spreading of the infection beyond the original site signals a serious health problem. A doctor may prescribe oral antibiotics. An earring that becomes embedded in the skin may require medical attention as well.

Because the skin is being punctured, a person is susceptible to getting a disease that is transmitted through the blood. Many piercers have completed blood-borne pathogen certification to meet Occupational Safety and Health Administration regulations. This verifies that the practitioners understand how blood-borne pathogens spread, how to avoid exposure, and what to do if a customer is exposed to infectious matter. The Centers for Disease Control and Prevention suggests that piercers also have certification in first aid so that they can handle an emergency, such as the client accidentally getting stabbed or passing out from fear or pain.

Blood-borne diseases, such as hepatitis B or hepatitis C, can seriously damage the liver. Research has shown that hepatitis B can live on a dry surface for up to a week—another reason why continued attention to sanitation is essential. An inflammation of the heart called endocarditis also may start when specific germs enter the bloodstream. All these conditions are potentially life-threatening.

A HEALTH CONCERN PRECHECK

A person with health problems may want to check with a doctor before going under the needle. The Association of Professional Piercers recommends not getting a piercing if one has:

- a skin irritation or an unusual lesion or rash, lump, cut, mole, or lots of freckles or abrasions where you want to get pierced
- diabetes, hemophilia, an autoimmune disorder, certain heart conditions, or other medical conditions that might interfere with the healing process
- a job or regular activity that would make having a piercing risky
- plans to become pregnant (or is already pregnant) and wants a nipple, navel, or other piercing

DOWN IN THE MOUTH

Because the mouth is loaded with millions of bacteria, oral piercings may be riskier than others. Oral piercing can also cause chipping to the teeth, interfere with speaking or swallowing, and cause an allergic reaction or breathing complications if the jewelry is inhaled. Tongue swelling from an infection could also block breathing. The tongue contains lot of blood vessels so excessive bleeding may result.

Oral jewelry can wear away at tooth enamel and possibly create a speech impediment. Not to mention that bacteria can accumulate around the piercing and cause bad breath.

SKIN REACTIONS AND SCARRING

The APP says that all sorts of bumps, lumps, and skin irritations can crop up around a piercing. The jewelry material, a cleaning product used, or stress from an inserted piece may all be to blame. Sometimes it takes some trial and error to pinpoint what is triggering a reaction.

Adornments in the mouth require special attention to avoid health problems. Tongue jewelry can trap bacteria, cause bad breath, and possibly make it difficult to speak, for instance.

A variety of scars can arise as skin heals. The two primary types are hypertrophic and keloid scars. The American Osteopathic College of Dermatology (AOCD) says that hypertrophic scars are more common. They

WHEN PIERCINGS GO WRONG

Most people get piercings and carry on with their lives without problems. A few stories, however, show how body modification can go unexpectedly wrong. In the summer of 2017, the *Daily Mail* reported that twenty-one-year-old Paris Mann had her helix pierced at a licensed shop, but it soon turned into a messy infection. Her ear was dripping lymph fluid and blood "like a tap," she said. The ear doubled in size, and a rash spread down her neck. She wound up in the hospital taking antibiotics. Doctors said she was lucky not to lose her entire ear. Similarly, college student Bianca Hart also described in the *Daily Mail* how she received an ear piercing that became so infected that she ended up losing part of her ear.

Women's Health reported on one woman who had a violent reaction to the piercing process itself. The twenty-year-old fainted and started convulsing as soon as the steel needle touched her ear.

In 2016, a teen acquired a gruesome infection shortly after having her tongue pierced. Soon following the procedure, her tongue started swelling and feeling heavy. It became so bad that she had trouble breathing. After she developed a blood-filled lump on it, she went for medical help. Doctors treated her for an infection and a blood clot, which saved her life.

The lesson here is to keep a close eye on every piercing and get medical attention immediately when signs of infection appear.

don't get as big as keloids and may fade with time. Keloids are raised, reddish, oversized nodules that develop at the injury site. They are considered benign tumors, according to the AOCD. There are also atrophic scars, which appear as a sunken recess in the skin with a pitted appearance.

PREVENTING SKIN TEARS

Tearing can be a worry, too, depending on what kind of jewelry a person wears and how thin through the skin a piercing is made. Jewelry can get caught on belts, bed-sheets, and other fabrics, and then sudden movement can rip the skin. Playing sports can lead to more unfortunate episodes when jewelry hooks and then damages tissue. Falls and accidents can also lead to a disastrous pulling of an earring or other piece of jewelry.

MENTAL HEALTH MATTERS

Although the cases are rare, a few people get addicted to piercing, and excessive piercing can be unhealthy and a symptom of some other underlying mental problem. A person can get so addicted that he or she overdoes it and continually needs "a fix." A statement published by the American Academy of Child and Adolescent Psychiatry viewed too much piercing as a form of self-mutilation on a par with cutting, burning, and head banging. It may be a sign of self-loathing, depression, or social alienation.

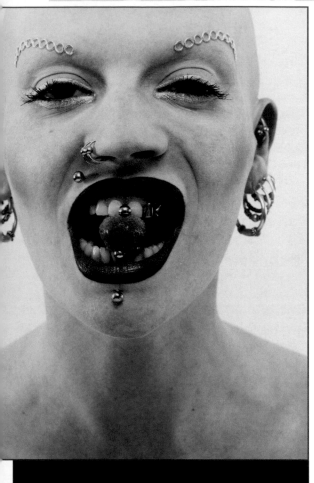

For some, excessive piercing may be a sign of a mental health issue. Too much body modification may be a sign that a person is depressed or experiencing inner distress.

If you're getting many piercings or considering it, you should ask yourself if you're exhibiting addictive behavior or if the piercing is negatively affecting your life.

While it's helpful to be aware of the negatives, piercing can still be very empowering for certain individuals—boosting a person's looks and self-esteem. They can feel that they now belong to a special group, yet they are expressing themselves as individuals. Piercing is a ritual that reaches back to ancient times, yet has been reclaimed as a modern practice for people today.

GLOSSARY

ACUPUNCTURE A Chinese medical practice that treats illness, relieves pain, or promotes healing by inserting fine needles through the skin at specific points.

ADRENALINE A hormone released by the adrenal gland, especially during times of stress, that increases the heart rate and gives a person more energy.

ANESTHETIC A substance that brings about a loss of sensation.

ANTIBIOTICS Medicines that weaken or destroy specific microorganisms, especially bacteria or fungi; used to treat infections.

AUTOCLAVE A strong, specialized container that uses high heat and pressure to sterilize equipment and supplies.

AYURVEDIC Relating to one of the world's oldest holistic (whole-body) healing systems, developed over three thousand years ago in India.

BIFURCATION A division into two parts or branches.

COUNTERCULTURE A way of life, a set of attitudes, or a group of people whose ideas and values are at odds with mainstream accepted beliefs.

DISINFECT To clean something, especially using chemicals, in order to kill bacteria that could cause an infection.

DOWRY Property or money brought by a bride to her husband on their marriage.

ENDORPHINS Hormones naturally released in the brain to reduce pain.

GAUGING Gradually increasing the size of a piercing hole to fit larger jewelry.

HEPATITIS An inflammation of the liver caused by a blood-borne virus.

KELOID An abnormal but benign growth of scar tissue that forms at the site of a skin injury.

ORBITAL Two piercings connected by one piece of jewelry.

SEPTUM The dividing wall between the nostrils.

STERILE Free from bacteria or other living micro-organisms; totally clean.

TOXIC SHOCK SYNDROME A potentially deadly condition, caused by certain toxic infections, that can be brought on by *Staphylococcus aureus* (staph) bacteria or group A streptococcus (strep) bacteria.

FOR MORE INFORMATION

Alliance of Professional Tattooists
22025 W. 66th St.
Shawnee, KS 66226
(816) 979-1300
Website: http://www.safe-tattoos.com
Facebook: @safe.tattoo
This professional group is dedicated to health and
safety issues facing the growing national tattoo
industry, including piercing-related concerns.

Association of Professional Piercers
700 Massachusetts Street, # 105
Lawrence, KS 66044
(785) 841-6060
Website: https://www.safepiercing.org
Facebook: @APPsafepiercing
Instagram: @safepiercing
This nonprofit is dedicated to distributing vital health
and safety information about body piercing to
piercers, health care professionals, legislators, and
the general public.

Canadian Medical Association
1867 Alta Vista Drive
Ottawa, ON
K1G 5W8
(613) 731-8610 or (800) 663-7336

Website: https://www.cma.ca
Facebook: @CanadianMedicalAssociation
Twitter: @CMA_docs
Instagram: @cma_docs
YouTube: @CanadianMedicalAssoc
This national, voluntary association of physicians pub-
  lishes a medical journal, which has featured several
  stories on health issues related to piercings.

Centers for Disease Control and Prevention (CDC)
1600 Clifton Road
Atlanta, GA 30333
(404) 639-3311
Website: http://www.cdc.gov
Facebook: @CDC
Twitter and Instagram: @CDCgov
YouTube: @CDCstreamingHealth
The leading federal agency dedicated to protecting the
  nation's health, the CDC provides information on the
  health risks of various body art practices for both
  clients and artists and how to minimize them.

Health Canada
Address Locator 0900C2
Ottawa, Ontario
K1A 0K9
(866) 225-0709

Website: https://www.canada.ca/en/health-canada.html
Facebook and YouTube: @health-canada
Twitter: @GovCanHealth
This Canadian government agency provides helpful
  information on getting tattoos, piercings, and other
  body modifications.

**University of Pennsylvania Museum of Archaeology
  and Anthropology**
"Bodies of Cultures: A World Tour of Body Modification"
3260 South Street
Philadelphia, PA 19104
(215) 898-4000
Website: https://www.penn.museum/sites/body
  _modification/bodmodintro.shtml
Founded in 1887, the Penn Museum is the largest university museum in the United States and one of the
  world's great archeology and anthropology research
  museums. This website provides a guided tour through
  the objects in its collection related to body art.

FOR FURTHER READING

Angel, Elayne. *The Piercing Bible Guide to Aftercare and Troubleshooting: How to Properly Care for Healing and Infected Ear, Facial, and Body Piercings*. Berkeley, CA: Crossing Press, 2013.

Bliss, John. *Preening, Painting, and Piercing: Body Art (Culture in Action)*. Chicago, IL: Raintree, 2011.

Cohen, Robert. *Body Piercing and Tattooing*. New York, NY: Rosen Publishing, 2013.

Currie-McGhee, Leanne. *Tattoos, Body Piercings, and Teens*. San Diego, CA: ReferencePoint Press, 2013.

Frederick, Jerry. *The "Nuts & Bolts" of Body Piercing: What Every New Body Piercer Needs to Know . . . But Nobody Will Tell You!* North Charleston, SC: CreateSpace, 2010.

Gafney, Genia. *The Art of Body Piercing: Everything You Need to Know Before, During, and After Getting Pierced*. Bloomington, IN: iUniverse, 2013.

Quarto Publishing. *Body Piercing: The Body Art Manual*. Minneapolis, MN: Quarto Publishing Group, 2010.

Szumski, Bonnie. *A Cultural History of Piercing*. San Diego, CA: ReferencePoint Press, 2013.

Wilcox, Christine. *Teens and Body Image*. San Diego, CA: ReferencePoint Press, 2015.

BIBLIOGRAPHY

Breuner, Cora, David A. Levine, and the Committee on Adolescence. *The American Academy of Pediatrics Clinical Report.* September 2017. http://pediatrics.aappublications.org/content/early/2017/09/14/peds.2017-1962.

DeMello, Margo. *Encyclopedia of Body Adornment.* Santa Barbara, CA: Greenwood, 2007.

Dodd, Sophie. "What It's Like to Get Your Nose Pierced." HerCampus.com, January 24, 2016. https://www.hercampus.com/beauty/what-its-get-your-nose-pierced.

Escobar, Sam. "Why You Should Never Get Your Ears Pierced at the Mall." *Good Housekeeping*, November 11, 2015. http://www.goodhousekeeping.com/beauty/anti-aging/a35208/piercing-guns-bad-dangers.

Godek. Lauren. "Therapy in Body Modification for Sexually Abused Women." Lauren Godek on WordPress, December 12, 2013. https://laurengodek.wordpress.com/2013/12/12/therapy-in-body-modification-for-sexually-abused-women.

Marshall, Wyatt. "The Therapeutic Experience of Being Suspended by Your Skin." *The Atlantic*, September 21, 2012. https://www.theatlantic.com/health/archive/2012/09/the-therapeutic-experience-of-being-suspended-by-your-skin/262644.

McClatchey, Caroline. "Ear Stretching: Why Is Lobe 'Gauging' Growing in Popularity?" BBC,

November 21, 2011. http://www.bbc.com/news /magazine-15771237.

Mercer, Marsha. "Explosion in Tattooing, Piercing Tests State Regulators." The Pew Charitable Trusts, June 14, 2017. http://www.pewtrusts.org/en /research-and-analysis/blogs/stateline/2017/06/14 /explosion-in-tattooing-piercing-tests-state-regulators.

Newman, Meredith. "Report: More Young People Have Tattoos and Piercings Than Ever Before" *USA Today*, September 20, 2017. https://www.usatoday.com /story/news/nation-now/2017/09/20/young-people -tattoos-and-piercings-report/686360001.

Penn Museum. "Piercing." Retrieved October 24, 2017. https://www.penn.museum/sites/body_modification /bodmodpierce.shtml.

Phelan, Hayley. "6 New Yorkers on Why They Got Their Septum Rings." *New York Times*, May 11, 2016. https://www.nytimes.com/interactive/2016/05/11/style /septum-rings-millennials-willow-smith.html.

Rubin, Lawrence. "Tattoos and Body Piercing: Adolescent Self-Expression or Self-Mutilation?" *Psychology Today*, July 2, 2009. https://www.psychologytoday. com/blog/popular-culture-meets-psychology/200907 /tattoos-and-body-piercing-adolescent-self -expression-or.

INDEX

ABOUT THE AUTHOR

Don Rauf is the author of numerous nonfiction books, including *Schwinn: The Best Present Ever*, *Killer Lipstick and Other Spy Gadgets, American Inventions*, *The French and Indian War*, *The Rise and Fall of the Ottoman Empire*, *George Washington's Farewell Address*, and *Historical Serial Killers*. He lives in Seattle with his wife, Monique, and son, Leo.

PHOTO CREDITS